BOOK 5:
TIRE, PARACHUTE ACTIVITIES

Perceptual-Motor Development Series

by
JACK CAPON

Editor
Frank Alexander

Cover and Text Artist
John Lewis

Published
by
FRONT ROW EXPERIENCE

Published
by
Front Row Experience
540 Discovery Bay Blvd.
Byron, CA 94514-9454

CONTENTS

Part 1
TIRE ACTIVITIES

Part 2
PARACHUTE ACTIVITIES

PART 1

TIRE ACTIVITIES

INTRODUCTION

Tires are among the most versatile, inexpensive, indestructible and easily obtained teacher tools available for use in the physical education program. They are safe, easy to handle and their shape makes them convenient for storage. Bicycle tires, being lightweight, are more practical than automobile tires thereby allowing for a greater variety of uses.

The tires can be painted in a variety of colors and when used with colored bean bags, children can toss the red bean bag into a red tire, blue bean bag into a blue tire, etc. Matching objects that are the same color develops visual perception in your children and reinforces the same skills that are used in a reading readiness program. Using color labels children can match the word to the appropriate colored tire thereby helping to build and strengthen the bridge between cognition and language.

Patterns of Tires

Tires can be arranged in an endless combination of patterns. Children enjoy designing their own patterns. The children can draw their tire patterns on a 5 x 8 index card. These task cards can then be shared with the class, who can arrange the tires according to the pattern on the task card. Their creativity is allowed to surface freely as they share their task cards with other children. The ability to record a pattern on a task card and then have another duplicate the pattern from the task card is a skill that involves basic visual perception and ordering. They are also involved in processing information at a concrete level, moving to the representational level and then revising the process.

Although this activity is part of a physical education program, it affects the total learning process. Younger children love to move. They need movement and if that need is stifled they are likely to perform less ably in other learning tasks. Research tells us that children who are confined perform poorly on intelligence tests. These activities can be used effectively both indoors and outdoors. Using tires in a movement exploration program encourages the children to expend excess energy and tension, thereby becoming more relaxed and happy. They become more willing learners.

Where To Get Tires

Used and discarded tires can be easily obtained at no cost from local bicycle repair shops or gas stations. Each child could be asked to contribute a tire and one day could be set aside for painting and decorating them. It might also be a means of involving parents by having a tire painting party on the weekend. Parents could contribute ideas for their use and even use them at home reinforcing the skills of dexterity, directionality, balance, visual acuity and hand-eye coordination.

To facilitate language development, children need to have the opportunity to talk about what they are doing. In an atmosphere of movement exploration there is a feeling of freedom. Children can talk freely about what they are doing.

...."Hey, look at me, I can jump from tire to tire without touching them."

..."I tossed this green bean bag into that green tire."

Success will endow them with confidence and as their language expands so will their ability to communicate their knowledge with others.

Verbal Challenge

The primary method of movement education is that of exploration and problem solving in response to a verbal challenge. The verbal challenges stimulate language development, thinking and creativity in planning basic body movements. Each challenge allows for creative variability by the child and therefore allows every child a degree of success. It is the instructor's responsibility to see the each child experiences success and feelings of accomplishment as he solves the perceptual-motor problems presented by the verbal challenge.

Suggested Basic Challenges

On the following pages in Parts 1 and 2, we have given you numerous "suggested basic challenges" for each motor activity. (The challenges have been written in the same kind of simple explanatory language that you might use with your pupils.) And we have prefaced each one with "Show me how you can:". However, other prefaces such as "Can you:", "How would you:", and so on can be used just as well. The goal or point is to keep challenging children to solve problems. The goal is to keep adding to their ability to make judgments and to perform in response to these judgments. The goal is to help children think and do and, in the process, learn! The teacher is constantly encouraging, praising and noting progress and watching for evidences of creative thinking on the part of the children.

Success

The evaluation of success is made at once by the child and as he adds one small success to another, one new skill to another, grows in his ability to listen, follow cues, and create, he becomes what each one of us would have him become: an alert, confident, thinking, sharing, creating individual, a whole person.

GOALS

1) To promote competencies in basic locomotor skills.

2) To promote perceptual-motor abilities, including motor planning, spatial awareness, body image, balance, laterality, directionality, hand-eye and foot-eye coordination.

3) To enhance sensory functioning--vision, hearing, touch and kinesthesis.

4) To improve physical fitness of students.

5) To provide fun and challenging physical experiences.

6) To provide opportunities to relate and interact with peers

GETTING STARTED

1) Tire activities need space so it is best to set up the activities in a multipurpose room or on the playground.

2) Set up different tire activities at several stations. Such organization allows each child to work at his own pace. It also provides freedom of choice and the opportunity to develop self-discipline and self-actualization.

3) Each station may have a manager--in the form of a volunteer, an aide or an older student. This will insure a higher degree of mental concentration as well as physical involvement.

4) The children should be encouraged to move from one station to another after performing and completing the designated activity.

5) Collect enough bicycle tires so that each child may have his own tire to work with. This allows for a creative movement exploration approach, e.g. "Who can...?", "Show me how...", etc.

EQUIPMENT

All you will need for "Tire Activities" are: bicycle tires (used), bean bags, and rubber balls. Some optional equipment you might want to use for a wider variety of experiences, although not necessary for a successful program of Tire Activities, are: cross bars or jump standards with supports, walking board, and jump box with incline board.

Bicycle Tires
Used bicycle tires with 18 inch diameters can be secured at any local bike shop. The tires can be painted several different colors. This gives a very stimulating visual effect to Tire Activities.

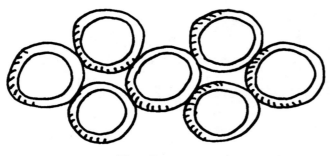

Tire Pattern

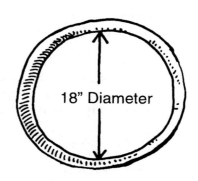

18" Diameter

Bean Bags

Bean bags can be made by parents and children. Children can have the valuable experience of measuring, cutting, and sewing.

Method:
a)   Use a heavy durable fabric like sailcloth, canvas, denim or burlap.
b)   Cut two squares of fabric 8" x 8", preferably with pinking shears.
c)   Stitch around the squares in a 1/2" seam either by machine or by hand, leaving a 2" opening for filling.
d)   Fill loosely with small beans or rice.
e)   Stitch and close the 2" opening.

You can also purchase "ready made" bean bags from the publisher (see page 36).

Rubber Balls

Use light rubber playground balls 6 to 8 inches in diameter. They can be found in the toy section of any large department store. There are also solid foam balls that bounce just like rubber balls do with the added benefit that they will never go flat. Both types are available from the publisher (see page 36).

Cross Bars (optional)

You can easily make cross bars yourself by using flexible plastic pipe or plastic foam tubes used to insulate water pipes from freezing temperatures at your local hardware store. Once you have the "tubes" all you need to do is get a jump rope or any old rope or clothesline cord and run it down through the length of the tube. (Or run it through the sides of each end of the tube as shown in the illustration, whatever works best for you.) Then you tie several knots on either end of the rope an equal distance apart. Once you've done that, in order to set up your cross tube, you simply stuff one end of the knotted rope into the top of a game cone on one side and the other end of the knotted rope into another game cone on the other side and there you have it! A "Cross Bar"! You can adjust the height of the Cross Bar by letting the knots out or stuffing them into the tops of the cones. The knots catch on the edges of the cone holes and easily hold your Cross Tube at the level you want. Also, another way to vary the height of the Cross Bar is to vary the height of the cones by using different size cones. All kinds of jump ropes and various size game cones are also available from the publisher (see page 36). The only thing you'll need to get is the tube or flexible plastic pipe.

Jump Standards

Jump standards (with supports) can be used in place of cross bars. They can be easily made from wood dowels similar to the illustration at right or the publisher (see page 36) can locate one for you made from steel poles which tend to be a little expensive.

Walking Board

You can make your own walking board out of wood from any lumber store by using our drawings as a guideline. You can also get a "ready made" one from the publisher (see page 36).

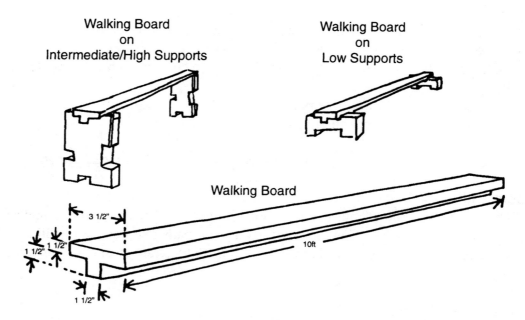

Walking Board
on
Intermediate/High Supports

Walking Board
on
Low Supports

Walking Board

3 1/2"

1 1/2" 1 1/2"

1 1/2"

10ft

1 1/2"

The notches on the 20 1/2 inch sides of the "Intermediate/High Walking Board" supports are for *intermediate walking boards* and the notches on the 11 inch sides of those supports are for *high walking boards*. Notches vary from 1 1/2 inches to 3 1/2 inches depending on how wide of a board you want your students to walk on. Supports can be made from a solid block of wood like the low supports or from larger pieces of plywood laminated to a smaller block of wood like the intermediate/high supports are. Commercially made walking boards (also known as "balance beams") come with high and low supports or they have an adjustable type support like the one shown here that you can make yourself.

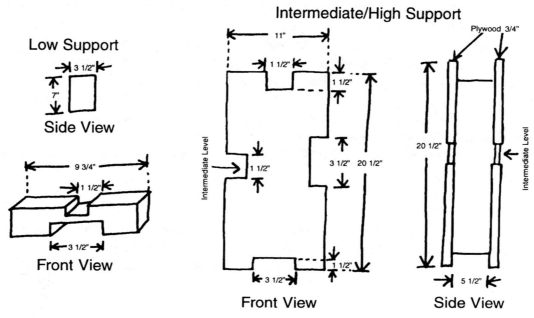

Intermediate/High Support

Low Support

3 1/2"

7"

Side View

9 3/4"

1 1/2"

3 1/2"

Front View

Plywood 3/4"

11"

1 1/2"

1 1/2"

1 1/2"

3 1/2" 20 1/2"

Intermediate Level

3 1/2"

1 1/2"

Front View

20 1/2"

Intermediate Level

5 1/2"

Side View

Jump Box With Incline Board

Like the walking board, the "Jump Box" with its "incline board" can be made out of wood from any lumber store by using these drawings as a guideline. Of course, like the walking boards, you can also order "jump boxes" from the publisher (see page 36).

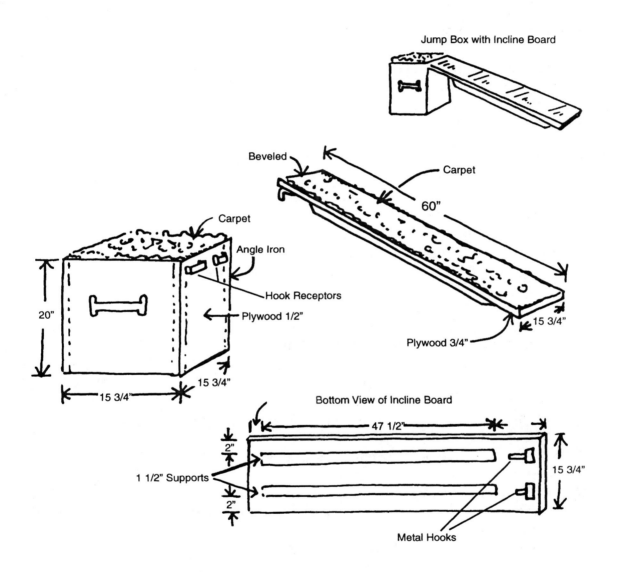

Jump Box with Incline Board

Beveled

Carpet

60"

15 3/4"

Plywood 3/4"

Carpet

Angle Iron

Hook Receptors

Plywood 1/2"

20"

15 3/4"

15 3/4"

Bottom View of Incline Board

47 1/2"

2"

1 1/2" Supports

2"

15 3/4"

Metal Hooks

1 BASIC LOCOMOTOR ACTIVITIES

SUGGESTED BASIC CHALLENGES

SHOW ME HOW YOU CAN:

1) a) put the bicycle tires in different places on the floor.
   b) move from one tire to another without touching the sides.

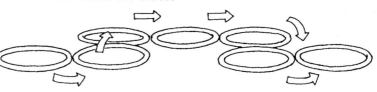

2) a) put the tires in different place
       on the floor.
   b) run through the tires, placin
       one foot in each tire openin

3) a) put the tires in different places on the floor.
   b) run on *top* of the tires.

4) a) put the tires in different places on the floor.
   b) put your feet together.
   c) jump in and out of the tire openings.
   d) do it again, but this time jump sideways in and out of the tire openings.

5) a) put the tires in different places on the floor.
   b) *hop* on your *right* foot in and out of the tire openings.
   c) *hop* on your *left* foot in and out of the tire openings.

6) a) put the tires in different places on the floor.
   b) get down on your hands and knees.
   c) creep through the tire openings by putting your hands and knees in the tire openings.
   d) do it again but this time creep on *top* of the tires.

7) a) put the tires in different places on the floor.
   b) go from tire to tire as a:
       • dog, moving fast on your hands and feet in and out of the tire openings.
       • bear, walking on your hands and feet. Go in and out of the tire openings by moving your right arm and leg at

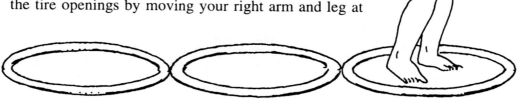

Page 8

the *same time*, then your left arm and leg at the same time. This is the "rolling" way a bear moves when he walks.

- rabbit. Squat down with your knees together, and hop forward in and out of the tires.
- frog. Squat down with your arms between your knees. Keep your knees spread apart. Jump in and out of the tires by pushing off with your *toes* and *landing* on your toes.
- crab. Squat down, feet close to your hips, hands on the floor behind your back. Raise your hips, holding yourself up by your hands and feet. Now crab-walk forward by placing first your hands and then your feet in the tire openings. Keep your body straight.

8) a) put the tires in different places on the floor.
   b) jump from tire to tire. Each jump change the distance between tires by jumping into tires a different distance away from you.

9) a) put the tires in different places on the floor.
   b) change the distance between the tires.
   c) run and leap into the tire openings, going from tire to tire.

10) a) place the tires around the floor in a pattern.
    b) move through the tires on three body parts, such as one foot and two hands, and so on.

11) a) place the tires in a pattern.
    b) jump in and out of the tires by doing twisting half-turn jumps.

12) a) place the tires in two straight rows.
    b) walk through the rows by putting your right foot in the tires on the right side and your left foot in the tires on the left side.
    c) say "right" or "left" as each foot lands in the tire opening.
    d) walk backwards performing the same task.

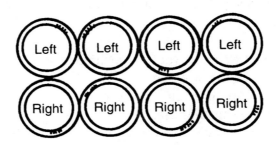

2 HAND & FOOT-EYE COORDINATION ACTIVITIES

SUGGESTED BASIC CHALLENGES

SHOW ME HOW YOU CAN:

1) a)   put the tires in different places on the floor.
   b)   stand at the starting line and toss a bean bag into each of the tires. (Vary the distance between the child and the tire.)
   c)   toss each colored bean bag into the tire that is the *same* color, red bean bag into red tire, and so on.

2) a)   put the tires on the floor end to end with their sides touching.
   b)   bounce and catch a rubber ball in each tire.

3) a)   place the tires end to end.
   b)   dribble the ball through the tires.

4) a)   hang a tire by a rope.
   b)   throw or pitch balls through the tire. (Note: This activity is excellent to perfect football passing, softball pitching and tennis ball overhand throw.)

5) find a partner, then roll the tire and let your partner try to throw the ball through the tire. (Designate which partners should roll first and which throw, then have them reverse the *roll* and *throw* roles.)

6) a)   place a small tire in a tire holder (or have an aide hold the tire).
   b)   kick the ball through the tire opening.
   c)   place the next smaller tire in the tire holder.
   d)   kick the ball through the smaller tire.
   e)   continue to kick the ball each time through the next smaller tire. (Note: you will need several different sizes of tires for this activity.)

3 MOVEMENT EXPLORATION ACTIVITIES

In the following challenges, each participant should have a bicycle tire to work with. The tire is placed on the floor or ground.

SUGGESTED BASIC CHALLENGES

SHOW ME HOW YOU CAN:

1) a) run clockwise around the tire.
   b) run *counterclockwise* around it when I signal (whistle).

2) a) stand in the tire opening.
   b) balance on your right foot.
   c) balance on your left foot.
   d) now balance in the tire on your right foot with your eyes *closed*. Don't peek.
   e) balance in it on your left foot with your eyes closed.

3) a) jump up and down in the tire with your feet together.
   b) jump higher with each jump.

4) a) hop 5 times on your right foot in the tire.
   b) hop 5 times on your left foot in the tire.

5) a) jump in and out of the tire with your feet together.
   b) jump in and out moving *sideways*.
   c) jump in and out of the tire moving *backwards*.
   d) keep jumping in and out sideways *or* forward *or* backward, mixing up the kinds of jumps in any order you wish.

6) a) walk *clockwise*, to the right, on the rim of the tire.
   b) change when I signal, and walk backwards on the rim of the tire.

7) a) run and jump into the tire opening.
   b) land *crouched* down.

8) a) *crouch* down in the tire opening.
   b) jump outside the tire.

9) a) stand in the tire opening.
   b) *long* jump out of the tire.
   c) turn and face the tire.
   d) *long* jump back into the tire.

10) a) stand in the tire opening.
    b) hop out of the tire on your right foot.
    c) continue hopping around the outside of the tire.
    d) change to your left foot when I signal and hop in the opposite direction around the outside of the tire.
    e) hop back into the tire on my signal.

11) a) place your hands on the ground *in* the tire opening.
    b) walk around the outside of the tire, keeping your hands in the center of the tire opening.

12) a) balance on one hand *inside* the tire, keeping your feet outside the tire.
    b) move your feet clockwise around the outside of the tire.
    c) change hands within the tire when I signal, and walk counterclockwise back around the tire.

13) a) place your feet inside the tire and your arms outside.
    b) move around the tire, keeping your feet inside and your hands outside.

14) a) stand inside the tire.
    b) make yourself *small* inside the tire.
    c) make yourself *tall* inside the tire.
    d) place your body in a position between small and tall inside the tire.

15) a) stand inside the tire.
    b) balance yourself with *three* of your body parts touching the floor inside the tire and *two* touching outside.

16) a) build a long narrow bridge by stretching your body across the tire. (Hands on one side of the tire and feet on the other.)
    b) make a vary wide bridge.
    c) make a drawbridge that goes up and down over the tire.

17) a) stand inside the tire opening.
    b) spin your body a one half turn.

18) a) choose a partner.
    b) stand ten feet apart, facing each other.
    c) roll one tire back and forth between you.
    d) roll *two* tires back and forth between you.

19) a) choose a partner.
    b) toss and catch a bicycle tire back and forth between you.
    c) toss and catch *two* bicycle tires back and forth between you.

4 MISCELLANEOUS ACTIVITIES

Tires can be used in combination with other equipment.

SUGGESTED BASIC CHALLENGES

SHOW ME HOW YOU CAN:

1) a)   set up an incline board with jump box (or a bench, chair, etc.).
   b)   place the bicycle tires on the floor following the jump box.
   c)   walk up the incline board and onto the jump box.
   d)   jump into the center of the first tire opening, then on through the rest.
   e)   jump into the tire of your choice.

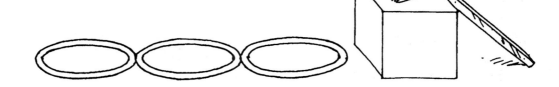

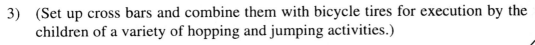

2) a)   set up the low walking board.
   b)   place the tires on the walking board.
   c)   step in and out of the tires while walking the length of the board.

3)   (Set up cross bars and combine them with bicycle tires for execution by the children of a variety of hopping and jumping activities.)

5 OPPORTUNITIES TO RELATE

Creating relationships in class requires many opportunities to practice different methods of choosing and changing friends. Several stages of social development are usually present in the early years of school. Some children can manage only one friend at a time, others can play with small groups. The intimacy of a friend helps a youngster feel confident that he belongs. Intimate groups of two merge to form larger groups and when that happens the child is proud that he is part of the class and part of the big world outside. When children work and play together in small groups there is spontaneous conversation, exchanges of ideas and experiences of acceptance and conflict. Good relationships thrive on communication. Children need opportunities to practice relating and interacting. Progressing from individual participation to group activities through individual exploration, contests, combatives and relays provide many such opportunities.

The activities on the following pages are specifically designed to provide your students with "opportunities to relate to their peers".

TIRE CONTESTS

The following challenges should be used with several children in competition with one another.

SUGGESTED BASIC CHALLENGES

SHOW ME HOW YOU CAN:

1) roll the tire and make it stop within the circle. (Children stand behind a starting line and attempt to roll the tire so that it stops in a circle painted on the playground.)

2) roll the tire as *far* as you can for distance.

3) roll the tire between the two lines. (Outline or otherwise indicate two parallel lines on the playground (floor).

4) a) place bowling pins in a triangle formation.
   b) roll the *tire* instead of a bowling ball to try to knock over the bowling pins.

5) use your hands to roll the tire between the two goal lines. See how fast you can make it go! (Establish an area between two goal lines.)

6) a) set up three or four tires in tire holders (or have them held up by aides).
   b) crawl *fast* through the tires without knocking any of them down.

7) a) roll a tire.
   b) straddle jump over the tire without touching it.

8) a) roll a tire.
   b) run around the tire as many times as possible before it stops.

TIRE COMBATIVES

SUGGESTED BASIC CHALLENGES

SHOW ME HOW YOU CAN:

1) a) place two bicycle tires on the grass or on mats side by side. One person stands in each tire.
   b) try to push or pull your opponent until at least one part of his body touches the mat (or grass) outside his tire. The one who pushes the other out first wins. Don't start until I signal.

2) (Designate a line on the grass or mat, and pair off opponents.)
   a) each grab hold of a tire.
   b) try, on my signal, to pull your opponent across the line. The first to do this wins.

3) (Designate a line on the grass or mat, and pair off opponents.)
   a) get down on your hands and knees, facing *away* from your opponent.
   b) position your body so that the leg closest to your opponent is extended upward from your knee and is touching your opponent's leg which is also extended up.
   c) place a bicycle tire over the extended legs so that they are "hooked" together.
   d) creep forward when I signal, trying to pull your opponent across the line. First to do so wins.

4) (For safety purposes use a mat or grass. Two or four can play this game. Opponents face each other.)
   a) place a tire over your head and shoulders, facing your opponent.
   b) put your arms across your chest and grip the tire tightly with both your hands.
   c) *hop* forward on one foot *only* when I signal.
   d) try to knock or bump your opponent off balance so both his feet touch the ground. First to knock his opponent off balance wins.

TIRE RELAYS

SUGGESTED BASIC CHALLENGES

SHOW ME HOW YOU CAN:

1) **Tire Rolling Relay**
   (Set up two or more relay teams.)
   a)   roll the tire down to the goal line with your *right* hand.
   b)   roll the tire back to the starting line with your *left* hand.
   c)   pass it to the next player in line who continues the play.

2) **Tire Carry Relay**
   (Organize two 2-partner relay teams. The partners carry the tire between them.)
   a)   race down, as you hold the tire between you, to the opposite end line and back to the starting line.
   b)   pass it to your waiting team members who continue the relay.

3) **Tire Shuttle Relay**
   (Each team consists of at least four players. Place two or more players at each end of the relay area.)
   a)   each carry a bicycle tire.
   b)   race down and hand off the tire to your waiting team member who races back with it to the starting line, etc.

4) **Tire Scramble Relay (Pull Over)**
   a)   line up behind the starting line on your team.
   b)   place a bicycle tire on the ground at the end of the relay court opposite your team.
   c)   run to the end of the court.
   d)   pick up the tire, pull it down over your head, step out of it, run back and tag the next player in line.

PART 2

PARACHUTE ACTIVITIES

INTRODUCTION

The parachute represents an exciting catalyst for movement in the physical education program. Movement means life. It means freedom, pleasure, communication and sensuous enjoyment. Inflating the canopy requires teamwork and cooperation. A child learns first hand the meaning of total involvement and so moving through space he gains an understanding of his physical relationship to the real world.

The games and exercises develop and strengthen arm and shoulder muscle development and at the same time strengthen wrist and finger muscles. There are wide variations in interests and abilities within a given group, however all students regardless of skill and strength can participate successfully and non-competitively, with the parachute.

A child must be aware of himself. With this knowledge he is better able to know where he is in space and how he can control his movements. This self-discovery is unique to each child as he explores the infinite number of alternatives in working out a challenge. And as he discovers himself, he will become more accepting of classroom challenges.

These parachute activities assist him in improving his sense of rhythm, his basic motor skills and his self-confidence; qualities which have a direct relationship to his physical maturity and his academic performance.

The teacher might also want to give the class a brief historical background about the parachute. This could prove stimulating to the children and perhaps would encourage the students to pursue the subject further.

The parachute lends itself to both indoor and outdoor use. Space permitting, it is a marvelous activity for rainy days.

Each child achieves immediate success and gratification. The removal of competition and the risk of failure create a positive attitude toward learning both in and out of the classroom.

GOALS

1) To improve physical fitness of students by increasing arm and shoulder strength and cardiorespiratory stimulation.

2) To develop a sense of participation, group spirit and coordinate cooperation behaviors in a group task.

3) To promote competencies in basic locomotor skills.

4) To provide all students with both a physically and emotionally satisfying experience.

GETTING STARTED

1) Place canopy on the ground.

2) Students stand in a circle around the edge of the canopy.

3) Inflate the canopy according to the procedure in **INFLATION** on page 20.

4) Team effort is necessary for good results.

5) Be specific about signals and use consistent vocabulary so that directions are clear.

6) Demonstrate the 3 grips:
   a) Underhand Grip (palms up).
   b) Overhand Grip (palms down, fingers grasping top edge).
   c) Alternating Grip (one palm up and one palm down).

EQUIPMENT

All you will need for "Parachute Activities" is a parachute. Optional equipment includes: rubber balls and jump ropes. You can get light rubber playground balls, 6 to 8 inches in diameter, from the toy section of any large department store. Likewise, you should not have any trouble locating standard playground jump ropes. Or, as with other equipment used in the activities in this book, you can get the parachutes, jump ropes and the balls directly from the publisher (see page 36).

To make Parachute Activities even more stimulating and fun, play "rhythmical" music as your students go through their activities. It can be chants, rhythmic sounds, or musical sounds your students make up or you can purchase specially recorded music for the parachute from the publisher (see page 36).

1) For a better grip have students roll the edge of the canopy toward the center 5-10 rolls.
2) Have students hold on to the edge of the canopy at all times unless instructed to do otherwise.
3) Have students carefully watch where they are going at all times.
4) Never allow students to toss a child up and down on the canopy.
5) Do not allow "horseplay."

 **GROUP STUNT ACTIVITIES**

The most exciting parachute activities involve cooperation whereby the canopy is inflated with air. The billowing canopy is a satisfying experience.

INFLATION

SUGGESTED BASIC CHALLENGES

SHOW ME HOW YOU CAN:

1) all stand in a circle.

2) grasp the edge of the parachute at a seam (overhand grip).

3) raise the parachute to your waist level.

4) bend over and touch the parachute to the ground.

5) bend back up and stretch your arms overhead to raise the parachute when I say: "one, two, *stretch*!"

6) bring the parachute back down, then up again when I say, "one, two, *stretch*!". Continue to pump the parachute up and down this way several times to gain maximum inflation. (Note: This stunt is basic procedure for many of the parachute activities described in this booklet.)

MOUNTAIN OF AIR

SUGGESTED BASIC CHALLENGES

SHOW ME HOW YOU CAN:

1) all together inflate the parachute.

2) take three steps *toward* the center of the *inflated* parachute when I say "In 1 - 2 3."

3) take tree steps *backward*, as canopy starts to *deflate*, when I say "Out 1 - 2 - 3."

MUSHROOM

SUGGESTED BASIC CHALLENGES

SHOW ME HOW YOU CAN:

1) all together inflate the parachute.

2) all quickly pull the edge of the inflated parachute down to the ground. This traps the air inside making a mushroom shape of the parachute.

3) do it again. Make another giant mushroom!

Variation:

1) make another mushroom, but this time take 3 steps toward the center *before* pulling the edge down to trap the air inside. (Divide the class into teams.)

2) keep the parachute inflated longer than the other team. First team (designate) take inflating position around the chute. (Time each team effort to determine which team wins.)

IGLOO

SUGGESTED BASIC CHALLENGES

SHOW ME HOW YOU CAN:

1) all together inflate the parachute.

2) all take 3 steps toward the center while the parachute is inflated.

3) quickly release the chute with one hand.

4) turn around quickly.

5) re-grasp the parachute on the *inside* edge.

6) kneel down placing the edge against the ground.

7) remain inside the chute until it begins to deflate.

8) stand up holding the parachute and duck under to the outside.

Variation:

1) count off 1, 2, 1, 2, until everyone has a number. Only number 1's can remain *inside* the canopy this time, while the number 2's are outside.

2) do it again, but number 2's remain inside this time while number 1's are outside.

SUNFLOWER

SUGGESTED BASIC CHALLENGES

SHOW ME HOW YOU CAN:

1) all inflate the parachute.

2) all take 3 steps forward toward the center of the inflated chute.

3) quickly bring the parachute *down*.

4) all kneel *on* the outside edge. (Chute should be in the mushroom shape.)

5) all join hands as you kneel on the outside edge.

6) all lean forward and backward as I say "in" and "out", like a sunflower opening and closing.

FLYING PANCAKE

SUGGESTED BASIC CHALLENGES

SHOW ME HOW YOU CAN:

1) all together inflate the parachute.

2) all take *one* step forward while the chute is inflated.

3) let go of the parachute when I say "Release!" (Chute should remain briefly suspended in the air before floating to the ground.)

GRECIAN FLURRY

SUGGESTED BASIC CHALLENGES

(Designate start and finish lines about 50 yards apart. Divide class into squads of eight players each. Assign half of the squads to the starting line, and half to the finish line so that they are in a shuttle formation. Start with the first squad at the starting line.)

SHOW ME HOW YOU CAN:

1) all eight grasp a front side (arc) of the parachute with your *right* hands only.

2) hold it high in the air.

3) run to the finish line when I say "Forward, run!", keeping your right arms up high. (The new squad of 8 is waiting at the finish line. They repeat the stunt running back to the starting line, and so on.)

2 CONDITIONING ACTIVITIES
(Isometric and Isotonic)

Children need physical activity daily if they are to develop to their highest physical and mental potential. The most beneficial use of the parachute is in developing physical fitness. This is especially true in improving strength and flexibility of the arm and shoulder girdle muscles. The following are the most popular exercises:

BICEP BUILDER

SUGGESTED BASIC CHALLENGES

SHOW ME HOW YOU CAN:

1) place the parachute on the ground.

2) stand around the edge of the chute with one leg forward and one leg back for good support and balance.

3) grasp the edge of the parachute with a palms *up* grip.

4) lean back holding on to the chute.

5) pull the parachute toward you when I signal, without moving your feet or jerking the chute.

6) continue pulling hard until I signal (6 seconds).

Variation:
   do this again using a palms *down* grip on the edge of the parachute.

WILD HORSE PULL

SUGGESTED BASIC CHALLENGES

SHOW ME HOW YOU CAN:

1) all stand with your backs toward the parachute.

2) bend down.

3) grasp the edge of the chute with a palms down grip.

4) each place one foot forward and your other foot back.

5) lean forward.

6) all pull *hard* when I signal.

Variation:

make this into a tug of war by each half of you trying to pull the other students in the direction *you* are pulling.

OCEAN WAVES

SUGGESTED BASIC CHALLENGES

SHOW ME HOW YOU CAN:

1) each hold the parachute at waist level.

2) wait for my signal, then shake the chute up and down and pull it back.

3) gradually go faster.

Variation:

all kneel and do this again.

SKY HIGH PULL

SUGGESTED BASIC CHALLENGES

SHOW ME HOW YOU CAN:

1) all hold the canopy at your waist level with a *palms* down grip.

2) spread your feet for balance.

3) all lift the parachute when I signal (whistle) until your arms are stretched as high as possible overhead. Do not move your feet, waists, or backs.

4) use *only* your arms and shoulders.

5) all pull back on the chute and hold it tightly until I signal (6 seconds).

Variation:
    do this again, but this time use a *palms up* grip.

WRIST ROLL

SUGGESTED BASIC CHALLENGES

SHOW ME HOW YOU CAN:

1) all hold your arms straight out in front of you and grasp the parachute at waist level with a palms down grip.

2) roll the edge of the chute slowly toward the center.

3) keep the parachute tight by pulling back a little before each roll. Timing is important. Be a *team* and all work together.

STRAIGHT ARM PULLOVER

SUGGESTED BASIC CHALLENGES

SHOW ME HOW YOU CAN:

1) all hold the chute at waist level with a palms down grip.

2) place your feet at shoulder distance apart.

3) lift your arms slowly above your head, slowly raising the parachute.

4) all breathe in slowly in rhythm with your rising arms as you lift the chute.

5) lift the parachute as *high* as possible.

6) all lower your arms slowly to the starting position, exhaling slowly as the chute lowers.

7) continue to raise and lower the parachute this way several times, breathing in rhythm with your rising and falling arms.

BEND AND STRETCH

SUGGESTED BASIC CHALLENGES

SHOW ME HOW YOU CAN:

1) all hold the parachute at waist level with a palms down grip.

2) all bend forward when I count one, and touch the edge of the chute to your toes.

3) lift your arms high over your head when I count 2, stretching as far *up* as possible.

4) bend forward at your waist when I count 3, and again touch your toes.

5) go back up in the same way when I count 4, come down again on 5, *up* again on 6, and so on for several times as I continue to count.

PUSH-UPS

SUGGESTED BASIC CHALLENGES

SHOW ME HOW YOU CAN:

1) all together inflate the parachute.

2) make a big mushroom by placing the edge of the chute on the ground.

3) all squat and extend your legs back straight in a push-up position with your knees straight and your hands holding the chute edge tightly on the ground.

4) do push-ups on my signal while the parachute is inflated in the shape of a mushroom. Lower and raise your body by touching your chest to the parachute.

MODIFIED SQUAT THRUSTS

SUGGESTED BASIC CHALLENGES

SHOW ME HOW YOU CAN:

1) all together inflate the parachute.

2) make a mushroom by placing the edge of the chute on the ground.

3) all squat down with your knees bent and your hands holding the edge of the parachute on the ground.

4) all extend your legs straight back when I count "1".

5) return to the squat position when I count "2".

6) extend your legs straight back again on count "3".

7) return to the squat position on count "4", and continue, legs back, return to squat, back again, until I stop counting. (Note: *Do not* come to a standing position as in a regular squat thrust.)

TUG-OF-WAR

SUGGESTED BASIC CHALLENGES

SHOW ME HOW YOU CAN:

1) all work together to make a long rope of the parachute by rolling it up like you would roll up a rug. (Select 2 teams. Identify the center of the rolled up chute. Place one team on either side of the center.)

2) have a tug-of-war with each team starting to pull against the other when I signal (whistle). The team which pulls the other over the center line first wins. (Note: the nylon parachute is extremely strong and therefore safe for this activity *when it is rolled up*, do not do this activity when it is not rolled up or the chute may tear and possible injury could result! Use a grassy area for extra safety.)

3 GAME ACTIVITIES

Many of the popular games which are standard part of our elementary school physical education programs can be readily adapted to use with the parachute, for example: *Circle Chase, Dodge Ball, Mouse Trap* and *Grey Owl*.

POPCORN

Participants line up around the parachute and grip it using an overhand grip. A number of light rubber balls are then placed on the parachute.

SUGGESTED BASIC CHALLENGES

SHOW ME HOW YOU CAN:

1) grip the parachute firmly using an overhand grip.

2) shake the parachute up and down making the balls bounce (pop) up into the air.

3) continue to shake the parachute trying *not* to let the balls go off the edge of the parachute.

BALL SHAKE

Divide the class into two equal teams.

SUGGESTED BASIC CHALLENGES

SHOW ME HOW YOU CAN:

1) grip the parachute around the edge with one team on each half of the chute. (Place a number of light balls--volley balls, rubber balls, beach balls--on top of the chute.)

2) try to shake the balls *off* the opposite side of the parachute. Do not use your hands to keep the balls from leaving the chute. (Award one point each time a ball leaves the parachute and touches the ground.)

SURFING

Participants line up around the edge of the parachute and grip it using an overhand grip. One ball is placed on the chute.

SUGGESTED BASIC CHALLENGES

SHOW ME HOW YOU CAN:

1) slowly raise and lower the parachute causing the ball to roll around the outside edge of the chute.

2) make the ball roll down and up like riding ocean waves and travel around the chute using teamwork.

3) keep the ball rolling on the parachute so that it does not go off the edge.

NUMBERS EXCHANGE

Have students count off in a 1, 2, 3, 4, 5, 6 : 1, 2, 3, 4, 5, 6 pattern. When the students have inflated the parachute as high as possible, call out a number. Everyone with that number lets go of the chute, ducks quickly under it, and exchanges places with another person having that same number. Students should get to their new place quickly before any part of their body is touched by the deflating parachute.

SUGGESTED BASIC CHALLENGES

SHOW ME HOW YOU CAN:

1) all inflate the chute.

2) change places when I call your number. (Continue to call numbers.) (Note: Penalties may or may not be imposed. This game is recommended for upper grade students. With extremely large groups, use more numbers so that fewer children are moving about under the parachute canopy.)

Variation:

(Repeat the game with such variations as having the children run, skip, jump, hop, etc., when changing places under the chute.)

NUMBERS RACE

Divide the class into two equal teams. Designate as team 1 and 2.

SUGGESTED BASIC CHALLENGES

SHOW ME HOW YOU CAN:

1) count off on your team so that each player has a number. Be sure to remember your number.

2) inflate the parachute when I give the signal. I will call out a number. The person on *each* team with that number will let loose of the chute and race around the outside and back to his own place before the center of the parachute touches the ground. The one who gets back first will win one point for *his* team.

3) race around the outside of the chute when I call your number and get back to your place before the center of the parachute touches the ground.

Variation:

(Repeat the game, varying the locomotor skill---running, jumping, hopping, skipping, etc.--- used in going around the chute.)

STEAL THE BACON

Divide the class into two equal teams. Designate one team as the *Tigers* and the other as the *Bears*.

SUGGESTED BASIC CHALLENGES

SHOW ME HOW YOU CAN:

1) count off in the *Tiger* team. Be sure to remember your number.

2) count off in the *Bear* team. Be sure to remember your number.

3) inflate the parachute when I give the signal. I'll call out a number or numbers. Everyone with the number or numbers I call should run under the chute and try to get the object that I will place under the parachute. Then race back to your places without being touched by the chute. One point will be scored by the player who successfully gets back to his team without being tagged or touched by the deflating parachute. No point will be awarded if the chute deflates and touches the player.

4) run under the chute when I call your number, try to get the object and race back to your place(s) without being tagged or touched by the deflating parachute.

4 BASIC LOCOMOTOR ACTIVITIES

Young children need exposure to a variety of challenging and motivating movement experiences. The parachute offers many opportunities for practicing and perfecting basic locomotor skills such as skipping, hopping, running and jumping.

SUGGESTED BASIC CHALLENGES

SHOW ME HOW YOU CAN:

1) all grasp the edge of the chute at a seam with your *right* hand.

2) circle forward to the left *(clockwise).*

Variation:

1) all grasp the edge of the parachute at a seam with your *left* hand.

2) circle *forward* to the right (*counterclockwise* direction).

3) circle *backward* to the left, when I signal.

4) move in toward the center of the chute.

5) move back out. (Note: Repeat the above activities stressing other locomotor skills: running, hopping, jumping, skipping, galloping, sliding. Also, marching is an excellent activity. Be sure to add appropriate music.)

6) make a merry-go-round by continuing to raise and lower the parachute. But at the same time every other student stand up while those in between squat down.

5 MOVEMENT EXPLORATION ACTIVITIES

Students are challenged to think and move in many different and creative ways. Listed on the next page are some possibilities for such movement exploration.

SUGGESTED BASIC CHALLENGES

SHOW ME HOW YOU CAN:

1) make waves using the parachute.

2) run in a circle, holding the parachute overhead with your right hand.

3) all hop around in a circle, alternating from your right to your left foot while gripping the edge of the parachute.

4) grip the parachute with both of your hands, palms down with arms stretched straight out, and raise and lower the parachute.

5) roll the parachute very fast toward the center, keeping the parachute tight at all times.

6) raise the parachute overhead, let go of it, and then regrasp it while it is still floating in the air.

7) cross your arms and pull back hard on the parachute while I count to 6.

8) hold the parachute at a high level while you all run at a low level.

9) do sit-ups while grasping the edge of the parachute. See if you can do 10 sit-ups in a row while grasping the parachute.

10) inflate the parachute and run to your left. Do it again, but this time, run to your right.

11) inflate the parachute and hop 3 steps toward the center and then 3 steps back out.

12) all get together and work out as a team some new stunt to do with the parachute.

13) pass the parachute quickly around in a circle without moving your feet.

6 SPECIAL ACTIVITIES

There are many special activities that can be used with parachutes. Allowing the imagination and creativity of children and teacher to surface can produce many possibilities. Listed on the next page are several that will enhance any physical education program.

TUMBLING

SUGGESTED BASIC CHALLENGES

SHOW ME HOW YOU CAN:

1) place mats under the parachute.

2) inflate the parachute.

3) take turns, three or four at a time, doing stunts *under* the inflated canopy, such as forward or backward rolls, animal stunts, and so on.

PYRAMIDS

Divide class into teams of 3-6. Each team, when directed, will leave the inflated parachute and attempt to build a pyramid under the canopy before it deflates and touches them. Allow teams time enough beforehand to practice pyramids without using the parachute.

SUGGESTED BASIC CHALLENGES

SHOW ME HOW YOU CAN:

1) place mats under the parachute.

2) inflate the parachute.

3) leave the edge of the parachute and build a pyramid under it before it deflates and touches any of you.

SELF-TESTING

SUGGESTED BASIC CHALLENGES

SHOW ME HOW YOU CAN:

1) inflate the canopy.

2) bounce a ball (jump rope, etc.) under the inflated parachute. (Also you can have children occasionally choose their own activity.)

LONG JUMP ROPE

SUGGESTED BASIC CHALLENGES

SHOW ME HOW YOU CAN:

1) roll up the parachute in the form of a long jump rope.

2) run and jump over the rolled parachute.

3) crawl back under the rolled parachute.

Variations:

   1) hop back and forth over the rolled parachute.

   2) jump back and forth over the rolled parachute.

DANCE STEPS

While grasping the edge of the parachute, have students practice basic dance steps such as the *schottische*, *step hop*, *two step*, *polka* and *mazurka*.

SUGGESTED BASIC CHALLENGES

SHOW ME HOW YOU CAN:

1) inflate the canopy.

2) do the (*name of dance step*) while grasping the edge of the parachute.

If you would like to see our free catalog of all of our Movement Coordination Activity Books, Kits and Equipment

Visit our Website at:
www.frontrowexperience.com

or

send Email to us at:
service@frontrowexperience.com

or

Phone us Toll-Free at:
1-800-524-9091

or

write to us at:
Front Row Experience
540 Discovery Bay Blvd., Discovery Bay, CA 94514
United States of America

CPSIA information can be obtained at www.ICGtesting.com
Printed in the USA
LVOW032349230112

265279LV00001B/2/A